Most of All the Wanting

Most of All the Wanting

Amanda Merpaw

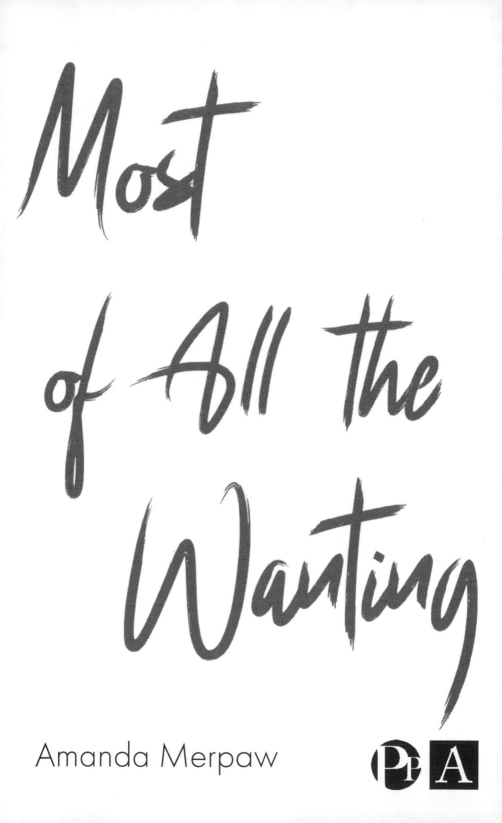

Palimpsest Press
1171 Eastlawn Ave.
Windsor, Ontario. N8S 3J1
www.palimpsestpress.ca

Printed and bound in Canada
Cover design and book typography by Ellie Hastings
Cover art by Alexandra Levasseur
Edited by Jim Johnstone

Palimpsest Press would like to thank the Canada Council for the Arts
and the Ontario Arts Council for their support of our publishing
program. We also acknowledge the assistance of the Government of
Ontario through the Ontario Book Publishing Tax Credit.

A **Anstruther Books**

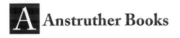

LIBRARY AND ARCHIVES CANADA CATALOGUING IN PUBLICATION

TITLE: Most of all the wanting / Amanda Merpaw.
NAMES: Merpaw, Amanda, author.
DESCRIPTION: Poems.
IDENTIFIERS: Canadiana (print) 20240359518
             Canadiana (ebook) 20240359526

ISBN 9781990293733 (SOFTCOVER) | ISBN 9781990293740 (EPUB)
SUBJECTS: LCGFT: POETRY.
CLASSIFICATION: LCC PS8626.E7546 M68 2024 | DDC C811/.6—DC23

CONTENTS

Any Closer to Grief

I Did Not Die

If Only in the Dark

Coniferous for You

For Tilly, who always waits by the door

Any Closer to Grief

What Eurydice Said to Orpheus, Imagined

You must realize that there are people
who have reason to fear. Do you

know me? A woman in the dark
might want to be left alone.

It's absurd how men always come
back. Won't you ever learn?

You have no right to love me here,
spin legend from condition.

I'm certain you're not meant
for me and you won't even notice.

How unbearable. Go inside
yourself and escape, repeat: silence

moves faster when it's travelling
backwards. It always starts small.

A bit of dark reveals us. I'm all
on edge, mirror and trapdoor.

Forgive me, I'm nervous.
I know frightening things.

Perhaps you expected some other
world. Will you listen to me?

People have been turned into pillars
of salt. I'm certain I don't want to find out.

On Being Gifted Thoreau's *Walden*

This is a dead reckoning.
The stars, do you see them?
They've taken to the fields.

Drop your midnight bricks.
What doesn't spark bites dust.
I yield my pulse. I knead it new.

Look, my finger, spun silver.
I tend to the tender of the wreath.
You're waiting in the woods.

We're on low land.
The foxes hunt.
I jealous myself. I forget touch.

This is an omen.
A gift is a world and it isn't.
We live thick lives and alone.

I forget what's indispensable.
Will you turn the fire, please?
Work prayers from pine pores.

There's a July reason I don't goodbye you.
I might almost say it.
I might almost.

Cancelling the Future

Don't ask how I forget about my body. My right arm. My collarbone. Both my legs. A buzzing between the ears. That summer at Grand Bend with the beetles. The generous menace of cumulonimbus. I breathed them into sentience. An owl. A rabbit. A bear. I told you, love is an accumulation. First here, then here, then here. We said we would sleep in the car. Did we sleep in the car? There was the rain and there was your face and there was my face. A matter of triangulation. The relative, the absolute, the relationship between. I position my feet. I evergreen myself. A heart is a heavy nest. My hands are spilling full. That summer at Grand Bend with the rain and then the sun. On the second day, the sun. The spirals bored into the bark. They warned us. Do you remember? I know you remember. I left my body to perch by the lake. Yes, the one that grows ghosts. I told her, the lake, I said, I always attend to an altar. You said I couldn't talk to water so I pretended I couldn't. Look, the sun. I freckled. Orion's Belt below my breasts. Touch me, I said. You wouldn't. So much fire is a way of being found.

Ode on the Unspeakable
after Sharon Olds, sort of

I come to see him in a new way now that I call him
to keep close and, having called, know he will not come.

We have sometimes felt exceptional, but in the end
we're left like the rest: someone says

I'm sorry or I can't or I almost want this
while someone else packs underwear, that good fig

candle, an unopened box of condoms, the alarm clock.
The only place to go together growing tired and strange

like this condo that night the winter fog
curtained our windows and we condensed ourselves

to its tenor, Joni Mitchell record skipping   *I wish I had a river*
timbered and desperate for the vapor to deceive

another street, and when it finally released us
he said, Look, even the air can change.

When we first loved each other we were convinced
this last hour was a long impossibility when it was obviously

just unspeakable. How disappointing if not gauchely
sentimental. After it's clear it still feels like July,

even now, like last July and the one before that and even
the one with the vows, binding our years to the carrying on,

I say to him, This isn't really anyone's fault, and he replies,
Don't make a fool of yourself. Why pretend this is something it's not?

Portrait of a Woman Leaving a Man Leaving Her

What else is there? The delicate world
made thin. The goneness
staggering, a gathering of shame.

Everyone knows Penelope
craved control, wove
and unwove, made present, made

bare, fibered half-facts, braided
herself broker of time undone.
Maybe all that remains is ritual,

knots of concern, ceremonies of self-
deception. Some demonstration—
an obsession, inevitably, with effigy.

Still, not a note pinned to the door
in sympathy, though gossip says
they do that somewhere, sometimes.

Not here. Best to leave a jar of honey
on the counter, away from open water,
to catch and hold our souls.

Notes Toward a Theory of Survival

When the future
          sells itself
     changed, stay home
               with your feelings.

     Time has to do with happening—
to be an opening
               and
               possible.

Arrive through probable.
Ascend through variables
                    of disturbance.

          Say *don't*.
          Say *doubt*.
          Say
               the shape of things

               and
                    the thing is not to burn them.
          Say *burn*.

Turn up wearing yearning.
                    (Yours, preferably.)

Inclination is discerning and
                    rebellious—
          a cistern of systems
               signing the moon's best phases,
                    the phantoms of ages
                              you haven't been yet.

Make a bet:
     who languages impossibility?

       Nature?
          Gods?

    An impossible me
    prodding past lives into knots?

Not likely or
       not like me,
       exactly.

Say *cyclical.*
Be typical.

    Be typically obsessed and obvious,
       obviously and obsessively
          a long surprise—
          a strike of suspense around the eyes.

Survive the world constantly
       if not carefully.

Survive the world persistently, pressing
          prophecies to bone,
          known propositions
             to the ground.

    Keep infinity recklessly close—
          secure your longings.

Writing to You from the End of This World

If poems really are
rapture—maybe
we're holier
than we think.

If I can make some-
thing real—
aren't I real?
And you?

Are we alive
like Emily
when she wrote
I dwell in Possibility?

I write it—
the everlasting
chance of our
gathering hands.

And this—
we are exactly
ourselves, ideally
and numerous.

Verses upon the Burning of our House

i.

No I didn't look for sorrow
(its silence) in the kitchen

ii.

I told you we dwelled
to one side of ourselves

iii.

Do you know what it is
to be overcome?

iv.

I took direction from
the crack in the tub

(you know the one)

v.

I revived the stopped press
I'll mind my ghosts

vi.

Yes
I lit the match

Stress Dream Diary

This morning: the coyote's skull,
pink blooms, black scratch,
soft paper. Forgetting. Once
it was fur, blood. At night
it pulled a leg from the dog.

Yes, it's new shampoo. Shea
butter. Coconut. That's enough.
Will you give the borrowing back?
A moment pressed stays
away. Say—that's beginner's luck.

Unsticking life from the corners,
the ones by the bathroom
with the ants dancing on,
too resolute to tread. I can't.
Stand back, I said. It's a dig.

Oh. There was that note you left
at the party. I saw you. We hiked
to the campsite. The huff
of a bear? It was the neighbour.
You laughed. I heard you.

Who is keyed to the hauntings?
The shapes in the shadows
still flaunt your face.
I cleaned my eyelashes
in the truck, dust clotted

the longest ones, out forest
way there. Did I clear these pines
for you? A hint to cedar
the path. There's too much bone
in that—I take it back.

Supermoon in Aquarius: An August Oracle

This is the moment of consequence. Don't be afraid. Offer healing. It's time to bend, to quirk, to tender to meaning. Evolve what's potent. Fruit your labours. Risk revolt. Remember: the cycle is pivotal. Here circle, here ritual. Carry the moon. Conjunct the sun. Still what's much, trust what's loose. Mend your desire. Defy darkness at the roots. Don't come dwelling—the day a delirium of possible, the night a discipline of delay, longing. Go on, collect implications. Count their teeth tomorrow. Today, touch what's close, closer, closest. There's no transit your body doesn't know.

Notes Toward a Theory of Otherwise

Days of happenings, now come

                                undone, done, sudden

                                         ly.

Beginning is a state of elsewise, elsewhere

    a start of birds and weather.

When I tell you I won't concede my life

    I mean

             there is much to say about living and time

                        is already now, a gesture

                                    of

                                    invention.

                                    I mean

                                    like myth,

                                    I mean

                                    a gesture of

                                    intention.

I wake up alone at J's place, Yonge and Eg, and feel unreal.

I wake up alone and feel meantime means meaning and maybe

I make mess messy.

Maybe

like most millennials, I'm obsessed

with what's possible, what's next.

What's left?

Imagine intimacy?

Imagine Dickinson: *If your Nerve, deny you — Go above your Nerve—*

Imagine yourself!

Look at me now, just look at me, above and alive,

denied and substantial.

Did I make a mistake and when was it?

Did I make a mistake and who knew it?

Did you?

Days of dreams and the thing is

it was you but didn't look like you.

I knew you anyway,

all ways.

I knew to insist on our tells.

Oh everlasting self, all I want is

holding, my own warm

fingers across my face.

I ask J, how does a person survive anything at all?

J says survival is beyond language,

all of us fold in on ourselves like

waves, waving some degrees

of

free.

J knows beyond survival it's phenomenal:

momentum is constant—

we move like light.

I Did Not Die

Aubade in Yesterday's Dress

I don't know how the curtains were drawn,
only that they're open. Outside,
an inundation of rainlight. Call it
morning. I dress cautious, watch my breasts
reflected in the pane. I heard what you
said, but I don't like to stay the night.
I know the shape space takes, how to say
thanks after I go. I anticipate the dark,
the backseat of a car, indexing stars
while my dog waits by the door. Where
do you feel most alone? Last night,
after the bar, you walk me to your borrowed
room, take the slow and scenic route
you've just learned leads you home.
I too love to linger below a bloom
of yellow lanterns, name trees looming
above. Last night, after the walk, you wash
a glass for me. Pour water to its brim.
I skim the edge, feet bare against
tile floor. Some languages surprise me
into longing. Some nights a clean cup
is enough. When I'm done, I press my thumb
to the back of your small teeth, hook
into the soft pulp of your cheek. Your bed
is as good as you said it would be,
and you in it. I like watching your tongue
touch what it means to work, to be taught
to want for nothing or anything
or actually everything. Everyone wants
a little. Sometimes more. What about
you? Have you enjoyed your life?
Me? I take my coffee gold and sweet.
When I get home I'll push my nose

into the beans before I grind them.
Fill a mug, let the steam clean my face.
There's a romance to what's ritual. You're
right, this is a lush street. I'm not sorry
to leave early. Look, the puddle near the lawn.
What I took for birds bathing are books
you left out on the curb. Did you mean
for them to drown? It matters how you care,
even in the beginning. I unlatch the window,
quiet now, hold last night's glass stained
with my lips up to the clouds. I let drops pool
on the pillow by your dreaming
head while I drink fresh sky water down.

Confessor's Flood

i.

Everything is ancient.
Monument of fate
burns firm, tender.

Bravery is a mistake
of make-believe,
fragments of love

wanting and sick.
Down the street,
everything is so easy.

ii.

Love said
survive.

The skin's glass
crooked

where I forgot
what it's like.

Hey—move
tender.

There's wolves
tonight.

Anything falls
behind running.

iii.

Strangers are dangerous.

Half the time I really try.

In the end, it was between

love and the party

        and love died.

iv.

Spectres like widows
toast vapor, disperse
weary and raised.

Truth, faster than you
and me, always slips
away.

Move like better
times are coming.

v.

We laugh at regrets
common as winter,

each one after another
weeds outliving their season.

I don't care. I'm holding
that feeling: all the love

we ever knew, kept
and hard.

vi.

How can this life hang on me?

Please, you know wonder.

When will I see you?

Will there be no one home?

vii.

Go see about the moon
crying
revelation:
    repeat it
      holy.

viii.

Suddenly
madness
can't
touch
time.

Drag
it
through
winter
dirty.

ix.

The quiet is in my pocket. The meddling night into the jaws. Not divine nor haze. Momentum for the sake of? For the sake of—

x.

Maybe you should never
dive back
to the too late.

Your body may be too
late, moonlight
in a thunderstorm.

Above the clouds,
the la di da di da
of maybe.

xi.

Here, I'm just a chain of relation.

Should my trembling own me?

xii.

Here I am the touch

around the air.

It's okay to over-

swoop, name what's

obvious. I come back

a fever. I'm still here.

Here I go again

                        with this one deer.
No, he never moves, though I eke
him into a line, maybe two
(then ten more), and he halts
like the time I first ever saw him
on Hanlan's Point. I swear. It was dark
and yes, unlit or not unlit but yes,
dark. The eyes adjust, as they do.
I don't know if deer exist here
on the island. I mean, how? You know
the island was a peninsula off
the bluffs, right? It split. Tore
apart. Explains the coyotes—
but stop, look, the deer. He's frozen,
exalted, or is he afraid?
I'm daunted by interruptions too,
especially in the shape of a body.
What's that? Okay, yes, there's been
at least one bottle of sauv blanc
tonight, chilled (of course) at the café
and talk of divorcing young.
Listen, nobody intends...
The deer! On the path, by the rocks,
no, those there, is he?
I've looked for him in every
poem since, even this one.
Shh! Don't! You'll—
I've never been so still, not in love,
not meditating, not even in
the kitchen mincing shallots for soup.

Intimacy Study

The poem slides into my DMs and says *Hey, how was your day?*

The poem knows that's a bad start, tries again, asks instead
What's your favourite natural disaster?

The poem is awkward in that charming way that really gets
me going.

The poem is hot and has good hair so I say *Well, hello to you too*
and also *I don't know, aren't they all a bit dramatic? lol*

The poem doesn't know its sun sign let alone its moon or its
rising but that's okay, we can save birth charts for later.

I ask the poem *Do you drink?*

The poem wants to take me to its favourite spot, a dive with
genuine ambience, a real mood.

I tell J about the poem, ask for help picking an outfit. J
suggests cleavage.

The poem arrives in a leather jacket. The poem looks good
in leather.

The poem likes to sit at the bar. Me too.

I ask the poem if it wants to share a bottle of wine.

The poem says *Sure, we can start there.*

The poem says I have a nice mouth.

The poem touches my thigh, wants to know about this one tattoo, and I don't hate the poem for asking.

The poem orders another round, Bulleit on the rocks. The poem doesn't ask if I like bourbon.

The poem wants to come back to mine and sure I sometimes do that sort of thing and sure I'm imagining the poem naked but sorry, not tonight. I want the poem to take me seriously.

The poem texts from the commute home and again the next day.

The poem gives good GIF.

The poem has zero chill. I dig it.

I ask the poem its attachment style. (Anxious avoidant, sometimes disorganized, obviously.)

The poem texts me things like *Good morning gorgeous!* And *What state of doubt tastes best? In your opinion.*

The poem is in therapy. Me too.

I ask the poem what we are. I say *So, like, what is this to you? No pressure! Just wondering, hahah.*

The poem says it likes me. The poem says *This is fun.* The poem asks *Are you having fun too?*

J says not to admit exactly how much fun I'm having.

The poem is good in bed. Likes to pull hair. Doesn't try to choke me without asking.

The poem says *Confidence is sexy, but so is your ass.* The poem tells me to put my ass to work.

The poem suggests a safe word and it's Wittgenstein.

The poem is a top. Sometimes the poem is a bottom. I guess the poem is a switch, depending on the season. Me too.

The poem asks about the best poem I ever had. I flirt back *Who knows? Maybe it's you.*

I make the poem perfect eggs, just how it likes them. (Poached.)

The poem wants to take me to its hometown soon but not just yet.

I invite the poem to meet J for drinks and the poem cancels at the last minute. I tell the poem *No worries, it happens!* I worry about the poem all night.

Back home, I text the poem *Hey, is everything okay?*

The poem says *Of course!* ☺ *Why?*

The poem doesn't usually use emojis.

I stalk the poem's ex on Google, Twitter, Instagram. (Okay, yes, even LinkedIn.) I send screenshots to J. J says *Fine, I guess,* says it looks like the ex makes bad art.

I tell the poem I'm fantasizing about it. *Yes, right now.*

The poem asks what I'm wearing. I lie to the poem about what I'm wearing.

The poem doesn't like bras or holding hands. I tell the poem physical affection is my love language. The poem says love languages are fluid, like us.

I tell the poem I'd marry it if I believed in marriage but look at the divorce rate. Besides, been there, done that.

The poem takes me on a walking date, says it just wants to meander—it doesn't want to end up anywhere. The poem tells me it loves my self-awareness.

The poem walks me to the streetcar stop, kisses me on the forehead. The poem has an early work meeting and needs to sleep alone tonight.

The poem starts texting exactly every three days.

The poem says things like *Good, yeah, just really busy with work!*

I says nobody is ever actually "really busy." Busy is a state of attention.

I stop asking the poem to make plans.

I call the poem and the poem doesn't answer.

I call the poem and the poem doesn't answer.

I call the poem and the poem answers all groggy, says *Sorry, I was just taking a nap. All good?*

I tell the poem it is not all good.

I make a joke to the poem about not wanting to be ghosted.

The poem says *Don't you know we're all already ghosts?*

I tell the poem it's possible to exhaust the use of metaphors.

The poem laughs and tells me to relax and take a joke.

I tell the poem to get it together, for fuck's sake.

I tell the poem it can be damn sure I'll haunt it forever as the ghost that got away. Who's laughing now? Ha. Ha.

The poem says *Woah, relax.*

The poem says *You're taking this too seriously.*

The poem says I should play harder to get. It's hotter.

I ask the poem why it said it loved me that one time.

The poem says it's not sure what I'm talking about but maybe it was drunk. You know how poems get when they drink.

I tell the poem *Don't you see? This is it.*

I try to make the poem cry. The poem tells me to stop embarrassing myself.

The poem says *Maybe we should take a break* so I say *Yeah, maybe we should.*

J says nobody is ever actually "on a break."

J takes me out for drinks, tells me to delete the poem from my phone, and I do.

J wants to take a road trip somewhere fun. Somewhere where there are no poems.

I can't afford a trip but we make a driving playlist anyway. For eventually.

At some point, on some pink morning when I wake up and think *I am better at being alone than I've ever been,* the poem texts *Hey, can we talk? I'm sorry about what happened.*

I know it's the poem because the poem likes to punctuate. The poem's punctuation is sexy.

I don't tell J about the poem's latest text.

After exactly three days, I text the poem back. I say *Oh, so you miss me, do you?*

The poem says *Don't make me say it.*

The poem says *Did you miss me?*

I type my reply a million times, finally send *I think I'm still a little bit obsessed with you.*

The poem says *Good girl. Now tell me something else that's just as true.*

The Melancholy

an erasure, with apologies to Louise Glück

I had a   melancholy
so melancholy it
        opened my letters, which were
                            answers.

                    At the outset,
when the phone rang,
                it came to me.

                    It was night
and the snow was falling.

Well, I said,
what can you do?

Life is enviable.

The telling of   days
and time,
and   the odd sensation
of   feeling something
for another.

It lit small fires,
I remember.

It was strange,
                as though
                        this occasion

        was radiant.

Then it was gone.

Outside, the snow
changing
        here and there
the street,   the trees,   white—
but   not really.

Leaving a Party in Kensington Market on the Last Day of the Year

This is it.   This
          & this:
the little
      handful of   you

& a little more.

Shall I mention
      the (gentle
          the)
          moment
          the sky
          surrenders?

Into indigo
      the smell of
          sweat
          & tangerines.

Look
      down Augusta Avenue:

      how   December
          is embarrassed &
          retreats.

If Only in the Dark

She Says, Meet Me at Pomegranate Restaurant, 6PM

And I'll admit, nearly nothing charms me
like the strut of a dinner reservation. I tell her
fruit is an obvious metaphor and she's all
Maybe the obvious is ours to spoil. Aren't intentions
a practice of kindness? We sit by the door,
knees coy and close, her hand pearled
with condensation from cold pinot.
She asks me my rising sign and
the saffron rice arrives swimming
in stewed split peas, the flatbread starred
with sesame. Here I am, a mouthful
of Scorpio, and now she knows. After rose-
petalled ice cream, she suggests that
corner cider bar on Harbord. I want her
to lead me blindfolded, desperate for descriptions
of the unfurling street in her mouth. Barely
in our seats, she kisses me and I already know
what to do with my hands. Touch makes me
material, mirrors me until I kiss her and think
of kissing her and think of being seen kissing
her. I allow myself to be perceived longer than
I expect. Did it take me a long time or no time
to get here? Regardless: it's now and real, my queer
ideal of pleasure, and no one, not even the rain,
has such soft lips. What I mean is, it was a good kiss.
Walking back to her place life-high and tongue-
giddy, she admits too soon that she wants
a family. I won't invoke the future, what I don't
want from it—not like this. Desire quiets
as much as it heightens. Later, in the salt
light of her room, sheet-sprawled and bra-
less, she says *I like you. Do you think this
could work?* Unsure what she's midnight fishing
for, I say *Who knows? Anything is possible.*

Letter to a New Lover

It's easy to become, tell little and turn wittingly,
which is not to say, by any means, it's not me
flanked by all my living, and yes, there are, of course,
those who disclose, refuse that mystery's the verge
of intimacy, but I'm not persuaded by precision,
there's nothing quite like tension, that distinction
of interest, that seduction where I eat my own tail, deny
it was ever there, and that, too, is a suggestion of love.
After all, what's restraint if not survival? Not apathy, no,
I mean the world is hard to reconcile with reality.
Don't you agree? You can call it maddening.
Even then, don't you want to want me?

Though Something Is Torn or Tearing, There Is This
a cento

Snowshoes, maple and seeds,
samara and shoot.
Me and my dog and
        an impossible view.

Bells have begun to notice me:
worn by salt and sway
in real time,
        if that's the term for it.

Either fiction or dreaming—
a walnut lets out an opera.
Something spills out my pores
        as light.

Essay on Memory

I return at the thaw. First fog of ferry light. There's always a boat, a body of water. Benediction carries itself the same. Can you stumble on grace uninvited? Once, there was mud. We wore matching boots. Not here, another lake, the other side. You burned coffee on the fire. The mosquitoes stayed the night. What bends in the balsam stays buried. The flooding, last summer, and again before that, and me too, flooded. After midnight, this clearing, that deer, I tell you, he hovered. Levitated. Or it was me. I was drinking drunk or I wanted to be drunk or I wanted to be impossible. I wanted to climb inside the hide of the deer. Me, in the ribs of him, held, holding. The galaxy. The swallow. I looked them up, the antlers. I didn't need to. The trees are different on purpose. Yes, they are. Note the nervation of the leaves. It's felt like change all year and now it is. Regardless, the lake is here. Keep your canoe. I summon the idea of swimming again. I told you, I talk water. I didn't expect to be gone and I'm gone. I'm full of moon. I'm full. Are you alive? I'm really asking. I should have been closer. I was close, but closer. The deer. To know. It's the hide, the humming. Today, it's Sunday weather out. I wear the wrong coat.

Portrait of a Woman Holding a Woman Holding Her

It is hard to imagine her face.
It was night, maybe she was spring-
cheeked. Both of us baring
some leg as the bars buzzed again,
patio season. Across Dundas Street,
the milky blaze of the AGO lobby
spilled out its last guests. She said
she loved *Middlemarch* better than
anything by the Brontës, would charm
Dorothea's rebellious brains out any day.
A kiss in the alley—did she start it?
She unzipped, held me holding her
without worry. Nothing happened next.

All Day I Dream About Desire

Some say pleasure is minimal.
What other dreaming enacts the world?
Excess is hoping, a praxis of surplus.
Reality summons body, makes time.

There are other worlds to dream, enacting
possibility. Gestures of longing start here.
Does the body make real? A summons in time
with ghosts already speaking, moved.

Who gestures here and possible? Start long
horizons forward and ecstatic,
speak moving to the ready ghosts, all
attention and traces of potential.

Oh, ecstasy horizoning! Ward what's
unnamed, always mutable and dawning.
Why attend to what's potent? Tracing
pleasure is mine, I say, and all.

The Communist's Daughter

Now is the time to talk labour.
We're here. It's Friday dark.

Look how the bartender lights
the candles in the jars.

I manifest this moment for days.
Who do you want me to be?

There's another set of eyes, of teeth.
Yes, red wine. You choose.

It's hot to be divorced so young.
To be so sure and sure again.

Tomorrow, the day after, maybe
Thursday, it's 2 or 3 AM.

You say it. We're haunted.
You say it just like that.

The table is tight.
Your hands right there.

They're real. I know. Then
there's the accent to consider.

It's July. It's been a year.
There's this nostalgia.

Can we first revolt in the body?
I forget myself. I touch your leg.

In the bar, I mean.
I remember to pull back.

Bring your brain along, it knows
something about rent, the market.

I'm thinking even now
how openness can be lost.

You kiss me outside the bar,
after the taxi. I keep walking.

Do you assume the future
exists before it happens?

I've seen *2001*.
I've seen *Apocalypse Now*.

It's the essence, isn't it?
A belief. An animation.

In my bed, you find my neck.
You're talking capital.

I wouldn't hustle like that
the rest of my life.

No, not like that.
I couldn't live like that.

Honestly, I'm impressed
with your connections.

You're clever. I like it.
It's your thing.

I race the rabbit hole.
You sleep round and close.

Can I tell you, this fantasy.
It's out there.

The main thing
is that it feels good.

Oh, you optimist.
You riff like jazz.

Keep talking communist
politics. We'll see.

I don't try to impress.
Not usually.

Put the ghosts down between us.
There's good,

next to the bottle.
We could order another.

Do you imagine anything
as more than temporary?

It's an apt question.
I'm absent already.

Reply From a New Lover

Hard question, not necessarily rhetorical: does your love
need to be metaphorical? Tell me what you like
and why you lie, the obsessions that attend you
to aliveness. What's best: being right or being lucky?
Being cherished or being charmed? Ten songs you liked
when you were young: go. You must remember someone
you hurt on purpose. What's worse: being embarrassed
or bereaved? Some people can't stand being self-
conscious, as if there's anything to do but fluster
ourselves. It's a big ask, but are you happy? Is there any place
you'd rather be? It's predictable, sure, but I'd rather be
on the moon, yes, right now, ancient and lofty and real.

It Wasn't Love I Wanted

My sheer white dress, your scuffed jeans, the summer
weeknight a luxury, whiskey and warm olives
in orange light, the idea of work exactly
that, cedar from your hair held
in the breeze:

> your thumb pressed the sunburn
> brewing tender above my knee

> and I let it—

Letter to an Old Lover, After Years of Waiting

I write to you from the other side
of my body. Do you remember my hands,
determined to perform in prayer?

I'm still aware of my palms, how they
fumbled benefaction, how my fingers
stretched until they cracked.

I'd be lying if I said I didn't think about
you, the scattered daylight in your room,
a hint of swoon beading your neck.

There were women before you but
I won't compare you to other women.
It's like I said, you're the only living girl

in New York. You've always had nothing
to do but smile. It's true: half of the time
we were gone and we didn't know where

and we didn't know when.
I still don't. Now here I am.
I'd be lying if I said I've missed you.

Do you remember that pizza shop on Main?
The day you held my hand beneath the table.
The fluorescent flood of fear consumed

your cheeks. I just wanted to have a Diet Coke
with you. I wanted to look at you more than
all the portraits in the world, no exceptions.

You were right, I picked the fight on purpose.
Sure, I hated your take on "Motion Sickness"
but I hated your take on me more.

Isn't that enough? Now we're both outside
looking through. Do you remember the bar?
You danced with that guy, a stranger.

Like you wanted to be watched.
Like you wanted to be caught.
You knew I wanted to want you regardless

of men, even when they enclose.
Don't bother checking for any more poems.
I'm over writing about what I took

for softness, what I took for bliss.
And was it? I could've sworn
we were exalted by the fact of ourselves.

Couldn't you tell I wanted to become myself?
I could've sworn I said it.
I wanted you to see me. I wanted everyone to look.

Essay on Closure

I try to end it the night we lunge lung first into the north country, the unappeasable shores of Lake Superior and me too unappeasable, restless and reckless, tensing the edges of the waves. We can't tell if they're advancing or receding. Gravity forgets us our measures of depth, the possibilities of proximity. You tell me to keep my distance, if only in the dark. Fine. I take to the trees instead, let my skin ferment astride a crown of paper birches. Peel back the trembling bark, bother a crane together with my sweating hands. Fold and unfold, fold and unfold, fold and let go, not looking where it falls. I'm not interested in persistence, how a thing begins and then continues. I thought you knew. Didn't you say you could press your tongue against time, clockwise my spine with my name until it stalls? *Oh*, you say. *Alright*, you say. *That's not what I meant. Not at all.*

Coniferous for You

Elegy Ending in a Toast

It's true, I can't remember
the last meal we shared.

Ghost of flour on the counter,
pink flowers centered, cut.

There was a list. Did you read it?
Even the wrong milk would do.

Dear ———.
Dear love, dear decade:

When does it end?
We do nothing and we sour.

We're off. Mostly memory,
cold syrah, crude questions.

I'll draw it. I'll start easy.

It was warm, right?
Southern Ontario. Saturday night.

Sprouts were sprouting
in the balcony's garden,

the orchard of our young age,
our old mistakes.

Were the peas good that summer?
Butter glazed in our best pan,

poured over gnocchi, freshly

forked. Thick yogurt, maybe

lemon zest, the chives
that always grew, a treat (or two)

for the dog. Most of the time
we were predictable as possible.

We allowed ourselves to be seduced,
knew all of time's discretions.

I couldn't wait. We made
this high, this hope, this hold,

this hook, this hurt, this home.
It would have been you

in the kitchen and you
with the toast, saying

  Here's to many more

or was it something else?

I raised my glass. I can't remember
if I was listening.

On Being New

The blackbirds have struck
all season, giving warning
to watch my head but how can I?
They're too small
to be this strong,
                    constant surprise
                    of puffed shoulders

and fanned tails. Those fucking tails.

It was the Commons, the path
below the park with that hot metal
slide, the swing where some kid got stuck
that time. The father a mess.
The ice cream
                    melted
                    down my hands

as I stared.

Do you think it chose me?
I felt close to being
something like
the sky, the patch
                    of grass where I laid
                    down with the dog.

I named aloud all the clouds I could remember.

Yes, even fractus. Do you know
any others? I swear I used to.
It doesn't matter. They're here
whether I signal them or not,
beyond my tongue.

> The bird, it buried its body in my hair,
> whispered in my right ear.

I wanted to tell you. I thought you should know.

Bar With No Name

When I get there I say to J I say how could we supernovas unfurl
so domestic it's not exactly like us J's all oh my god yes being an
adult is a real game-changer how typical we live kinned J's right
and perfect it's September we're in this equinox together it's true
escalation can undo you can't it and the bartender is like what
are you two babes doing in a dive like this and we lose it we're
easy so I say dying clearly (if you know you know and he knows)
J picks Lorde on the jukebox *Melodrama* what else everyone I
mean everyone sings along it feels forever eternally right here
this now relief we're losing it galaxies entire burning beyond rail
Rilke's right we must change our lives really J static will breach
beast beat us matter us mired moot myth J's like Haraway says
life is a window of vulnerability a function of possibility let's
disassemble reassemble regrown renewed like universes thriving
wild multiplied

It's Like What I Said in Therapy

There's a limit to my generosity.
My baseline theory isn't ready
but I'm on it.

What happened exactly?
You want to chart the conjunction
of you and me and

apprehension, how we came to be
eclipsed in just this way?
For starters, I feel shame.

When I concatenate the ways I draw
disaster, I don't deny
the blatant pattern. It tracks.

I've known since that quiz night
meeting your friends for the first time
when I spilled lager across the table

onto their laps.
You laughed when we lost
because I forgot

what abyssalpelagic meant,
though you told everyone I'd know words
and how to use them.

Maybe someone else should care about
the abyss.
The bottomless ocean.

On the way back to your place,
you pointed out
the digging squirrels—a sure sign

of a turn, you said, bring a coat
next time,
brisk nights are coming.

Then, worst of all, in the midnight
of your room, I stood embarrassed
by your kindness, how you parted

my hair to reach my necklace clasp, let
the chain pool easy on your dresser,
removed your glasses, kissed my shoulder

to your soft mouth.
You're telling me you've never been
devastated by sincerity?

You held me from behind,
caught my eye in the closet mirror.
We were not yet naked, your hands grasped

for nothing.
You said, we could be so good,
isn't that something?

Before Winter Rain
after Raina Maria Rilke

Suddenly, all around you, the cirrus sky
has disappeared. You watch the dog
creeping closer to the back door,
barking into the silence. From the nearby kitchen

you smell roses swooning in a milk glass
vase, reminding you of pear and Gruyère
left exposed, too close to that one grate
where the fierce mice pour in.

The walls, with their ancient joints, glide
toward us, cautiously, as though
they can hear what we are saying.

And reflected in scratched hardwood now,
the memory of sunlight, the nimbostratus
hours when you tell yourself not to be afraid.

Rhizomatic Thinking

We're drinking coffee in January's
bed. It's raining. The harbour
hammers high at Lake Ontario.
What an inconvenience. The end
times, I mean. Can I unwelcome
the undoing? There's burning beyond
the cusp of our cups. All of it,
actually, on fire. Last year I learned
to love a woman. It's softer.
What do you carry? I'm a tree.
The tree is me. Listen, I'm short
on soil, breathing breath, watered
water. I'm scarred down to the bark,
the branches, the mosses. What part
of your body would you most want
to save from extinction? Yes, you
have to choose. We've just stopped
seeing other people. Look at us
emboldened. I know I promised
to stop sweet talking dystopia.
See the sun? Me neither. It's stuck
in the cedar, it swells my molars.
The seeds. I can show you a forest
sprouting in my back teeth. I can be
coniferous for you. Even here,
like this. The astronomers, do you
know them? They say the universe
expands too fast. I get it. I quicken
at the quickening. You pour Québec
syrup in my coffee. Swoon. You
woo me. Soon we will coo calamity.
I'd rather my lips stick smooth.
To be an alarmist and all, the source

of this system we're melting
makes moves to melt us back. Scatter
the matter of our minds. So I prophet
doom where I see it, even sweating
in your white sheets on this winter
solstice. A doom is a doom is a doom
is a doom. How can my spine be of use?
You say if everything is ending,
everything is also possible. Look,
I pressed a bouquet of cilantro
into these pages. The stems glow
so green. What now? I want to wake
and world alive like this, like we're
at the Berkeley Street Theatre waiting
for the first blackout, the beat
before the play begins, where you brush
my hand and anything can happen.
I tell you, I say, if only I could think
of a deer, see antlers sprout across
the air. Do you remember? From
the trail. After midnight. You weren't
there. Yes, I should have been asleep.
Everywhere the night smelled
like dandelion fluff, like that pale dust
off Lake Ontario. It was an August
or two ago now. Maybe even three.

Scenic Postcard from the Rideau Lake Locks

His birthday and we make off again to the water.
Morning walk: we find a beaver in the boathouse. It's dying.
I google, of course: Are beavers dangerous?
He assures me they are, not to approach. I can't stop
watching, nearly make myself sick with staring, blinkless.
There are times I'm afraid to admit anything,
stand still to keep from doing something else.
After, I text the Airbnb host who says she'll look
but she won't know what to do. We're all useless here,
soft platitudes, leave whatever we want to leave
behind. Be careful, I tell her, it's got teeth.
Because it's still his birthday, I cook risotto from scratch,
sear mushrooms in a rusted pan, turn *The Crown* on
in the background so we can shit-talk the monarchs
while we binge-watch. When it's later and late and I
can't sleep because I can't forget the almost deadness,
I worry—what is danger if not an invitation?

Sunday

It's an endless kind of Sunday, the first one
of the month. At the Green Mountain Market
you make off with the basket, call me over
to judge petunias: yellow or white? The sun
precise and souring my eyes. How good
of you to want me kneeling near the basil
plants, my hands empty and open
and faintly citric. Love, I was full of it
last night when, half a bottle of riesling in,
I asked if you were thinking of someone
else. Even the moon's first quarter knew it.
Now we're here, clear as cloud, your shirt split
at the pits, cheeks flush with early heat. From
a film of shade I trace your brows, your
knees, your sandals stained with summer.
Sweating, you move on to the mint.

Essay on Me, You, Sure

What calls? Rest your stems. The fusing fuse. The reaching reach. Did you finish the coffee and leave the pot empty? Something about tired. I'm tired. I shake. Don't melt. I'll make more. I mistook a mistake for memory, momenting the moment at the pollen. I'm water soft. Smocked with mud. I simmer my shivers. I'm ancient. Who's telling? Tell. Tell it. Tell who? Me. You. Sure, I burnt the pie. Maybe it was on purpose. Once, you dropped it, served it anyway. In the stone house with the blue porch on the river. The St. Lawrence. Who's counting what counts? What's counting? We're not even. Assure me an assurance. Speculate a speculation. Possible a possibility. The universe is hardly constant. I dig. You dig. We're digging. Check my roots. Root me here. Meet me outside. Latch the intimate light. It's Monday. 5AM. There's moss in my mouth. I measure it. I mean it. I grow growing. I'm long longing.

Play the Way You Feel It

I say marigold

    you bloom around it

        this bruise on your thigh

            these weeds from your belly

                you can know you are entangled

                  you jump I breach the crease

                    of graffiti down a side street

                      in Parkdale we shoot storms of tequila

                      you are a clap of thunder

                          I am hurricaning through the crowd

                            we spin with Stevie Nicks here we go

                    again there is all this sweat

                there are all these bodies I know

            how wonder shapes the morning

          it can be Wednesday

        there is this precision

        this grace this kindness

of cirrostratus a relay of reaching

palms up to the abyss

where we exist

I must scream

I must stop screaming

On Being Plenty

Suppose we agree vastness devotes us to incongruities, a miscellany
of resistances to done deals, the specificities of facts. What's free
about nonstop emergencies? Patent flirting with refusals, webs
of futuring beyond signs? Speech acts of yes yes yes yes yes yes
and an urgency of what's at stake, agency close to atmospheres,
accumulations of articulations and love, too, a magnetic field.

Yes! It's true. I want it all and most of all the wanting. I cherish
ostentatious beginnings, harness the continuum of frequent
spectacular potentials. Love! I offer this incoherence, these impulses,
filaments electrified with graspings. Suppose we agree a practice
of multiplicity gestures to propulsions, rituals of self-constructions,
intimate correspondences turning towards infinities?

Summer Solstice
after Alex Dimitrov

There's an apt word for the length of the sun
and he names it, finds me there
late, in late evening light. He says
the sun can become, and can it?
My students, stubborn listeners, they ask,
worry: do you know the sun will kill us all?
Or its absence. Something like that.
It could explode. Or implode.
That's sort of the same thing, right?
Both ways a becoming. Not today.
Today I go in and out of the day,
this stretched and limber tilt of a day,
of a night. Today I'm here. I echo
my echoing. I spiral my spiraling.
He says love is hard to account for and it is.
There's duration. There's waiting it out
where everything is seen, can be seen,
where I see, you see, we all see in all
this daylight. Let's not account for our love.
Let's not count our love. We don't have
to do hard things because we can.
Leave that to the sun. Let's instead
be easy. Like the yellow towel
your daughter drops in the sand,
near the lake. She doesn't think much about it.
There it is, between us and Lake Erie.
Next to her falling sandcastle and my buried feet.

Notes

The section titles "Any Closer to Grief" and "I Did Not Die" are borrowed from Mary Oliver's "Heavy."

"What Eurydice Said to Orpheus, Imagined" incorporates lines from Jean Cocteau's *Orphée*.

"Cancelling the Future" borrows its title from Mark Fisher's *Ghosts of My Life: Writings on Depression, Hauntology and Lost Futures*.

"Ode on the Unspeakable" opens with a variation on the opening lines from Sharon Olds' "Unspeakable." This poem also references Joni Mitchell's "River."

"Writing to You from the End of This World" references Emily Dickinson's "I dwell in Possibility (466)."

"Verses upon the Burning of our House" borrows its title and opens with a variation on the opening lines from Anne Bradstreet's "Verses upon the Burning of our House, July 10th, 1666."

"Notes Toward a Theory of Otherwise" references Emily Dickinson's "If your Nerve, deny you (292)."

"Confessor's Flood" is an erasure of the lyrics to Neko Case's album *Fox Confessor Brings the Flood*.

"The Melancholy" is an erasure of Louise Glück's "The Melancholy Assistant."

"Though Something Is Torn or Tearing, There Is This" is a cento composed of lines borrowed from Donika Kelly, Barbara Ras, Ada Limon, boygenius, Victoria Chang, Adrienne Rich, Karen Solie, Feist, Gillian Sze, and Aisha Sasha John.

"All Day I Dream About Desire" incorporates language from José Esteban Muñoz's *Cruising Utopia: The Then and There of Queer Futurity.*

"Letter to an Old Lover, After Years of Waiting" incorporates lines from Simon & Garfunkel's "The Only Living Boy in New York," Frank O'Hara's "Having a Coke with You," and Phoebe Bridgers' "Motion Sickness."

"Bar With No Name" references lines from Rainer Maria Rilke's "The Archaic Torso of Apollo" and from various works by Donna Haraway.

"Before Winter Rain" is inspired by and borrows language from Rainer Maria Rilke's "Before Summer Rain."

"Play the Way You Feel It" borrows its title from Fleetwood Mac's "Dreams."

"Summer Solstice" borrows its title and some language from Alex Dimitrov's poem of the same name.

Acknowledgements

Thank you to the editors of the following publications, where some of these poems first appeared, sometimes in earlier versions:

Arc Poetry Magazine: "On Being Gifted Thoreau's Walden," "Summer Solstice," and "Aubade in Yesterday's Dress," which was also shortlisted for Arc's 2022 Poem of the Year contest.

carte blanche: "The Melancholy"

CV2: "Play the Way You Feel It"

League of Canadian Poets: "Essay on Memory" (as "On the Spring Equinox")

long con magazine: "Confessor's Flood"

The Maynard: "Verses upon the Burning of our House"

Plenitude: "Essay on Closure"

Earlier versions of some of these poems were previously published in the chapbook *Put the Ghosts Down Between Us* (Anstruther Press, 2021).

Some of these poems were prompted by or revised within the context of workshops led by Ellen Bass, Chen Chen, Ben Fama, Richie Hofmann, Annick MacAskill, Elizabeth Metzger, Hoa Nguyen, Karen Solie, and Bianca Stone. I am grateful for the spaces these poets created to invite conversation, connection, and communal learning.

I wrote most of this book at home in Toronto, Ontario, which is covered by Treaty 13. I am especially grateful to have worked on these poems while in residence at Artscape Gibraltar Point on Toronto Islands, which are called Mnisiing in Anishinaabemowin and which have long been considered a sacred place of healing and ceremony for the Mississaugas of the Credit First Nation.

Thank you to Ellie Hastings for the cover design, and to Alexandra Levasseur for the artwork featured on the cover.

Thank you to Aimée Parent Dunn and Palimpsest Press for welcoming me into the fold and making this book possible.

To Jim Johnstone, generous editor, mentor, and friend, thank you for your enthusiastic support of my work from your earliest encounters with it.

Finally, thank you to the Canada Council for the Arts, the Ontario Arts Council, and the Toronto Arts Council, for funding that supported me through the writing of this collection.

Photo Credit: sarah bodri

Amanda Merpaw (she/her) is a writer, editor, and educator. She is the author of the chapbook *Put the Ghosts Down Between Us* (2021), and her poetry, playwriting, and nonfiction have appeared in *Arc Poetry Magazine, carte blanche, CV2, Grain, Prairie Fire, Plenitude,* with Playwrights Canada Press, and elsewhere. Amanda was a finalist for *Arc Poetry Magazine's* 2022 Poem of the Year contest. She is currently a contributing editor at *Arc Poetry Magazine* and a member of the editorial board at Anstruther Press. *Most of All the Wanting* is her first full-length collection.